AMERICAN MILITARY INSIGNIA

AMERICAN MILITARY INSIGNIA

WILLIAM FOWLER

MALLARD PRESS

MALLARD PRESS

An imprint of BDD Promotional
Book Company, Inc.,
866 Fifth Avenue,
New York, N.Y. 10103

Mallard Press and its accompanying design and
logo are trademarks of BDD Promotional Book
Company, Inc.

First published in the United States of America in
1990 by the Mallard Press

ISBN 0-792-45079-5

A QUINTET BOOK

This book was designed and produced by
Quintet Publishing Limited
6 Blundell Street
London N7 9BH

Creative Director: Peter Bridgewater
Art Director: Ian Hunt
Designer: Nicki Simmonds
Project Editor: Shaun Barrington
Editor: James McCarter

Typeset in Great Britain by
Central Southern Typesetters, Eastbourne
Manufactured in Hong Kong by
Regent Publishing Services Limited
Printed in Hong Kong by
Leefung-Asco Printers Limited

▌ C O N T E N T S ▌

INTRODUCTION

An 82nd Airborne soldier applies camouflage to a fellow
soldier during training in the Honduras. The subdued AA
patch and airborne tab can be seen on the shoulder of
the soldier on the right of the photograph.

The unit cloth patch on soldiers' uniforms is over 125 years old. It was born in 1862 in the American Civil War, when General Philip A. Kearney, the hard driving commander of the Federal Third Corps, assigned badges to the divisions within his corps. This was prompted, it was said, by an occasion when he mistook some officers for men of his corps and reprimanded them about their appearance. The patches worn by the Third Corps were made from cloth cut in a variety of shapes. Some of this design simplicity still exists: for example, in the red diamond patch of the 5th Infantry Division, once the patch of the 1st Division of the 5th Corps in the Civil War. The 6th and 28th Infantry Divisions in the modern US Army also retain a similar geometric simplicity. Up to World War II the 1st Corps had their original round patch and the 24th Corps a heart-shaped one.

Within a year of their introduction, Corps patches had been adopted by all the Northern armies and General Hooker had assigned colors to the divisions within each Corps. The Civil War had begun with many regiments sporting colorful uniforms, but by its close these were greatly simplified and blue and gray had become standard colors. Patches were therefore a useful way of distinguishing men and their units.

US soldiers stand beside their French 240mm trench mortar at Vitrey, Meurthe-et-Moselle, 21 November 1918. An officer in service dress is on the left, but most men have simple working fatigues.

However, even today the US Army retains some of the old traditions of the 1860s, with colored piping and backings on modern dress blue uniforms. The infantry have light blue, the cavalry yellow, the artillery red, and engineers white. This light blue color appears as the backing to the Expert and Combat Infantryman's badge. The tradition is still remembered in slang — the pejorative nickname for non-airborne soldiers in the US Army is 'Legs' — an abbreviation of 'Red Legs', the term which was used for artillerymen in the Civil War because of their red or red-piped trousers.

The 'shoulder patch' as it is worn today was officially introduced into the US Army in 1918. That summer, soldiers of the 81st Infantry Division embarking at Hoboken, New Jersey, wore a hand-embroidered 'wild cat' badge on the upper left arm. When they arrived in France other US Army units adopted the idea, even though it was still unofficial. Permission to wear the insignia was given on October 19, 1918.

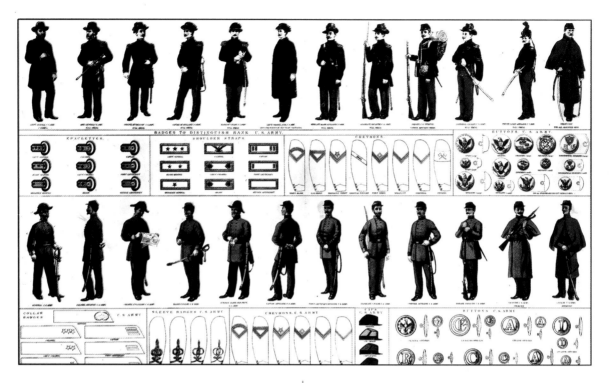

Regulation uniforms of the Civil War were more or less the same for both sides. The Confederate army was created, mostly by West Point graduates, on the same pattern as the United States army.

Though some of these badges still exist today in concept or design, many were created for the duration of World War I only and disappeared when the units were disbanded.

The Civil War origins of the unit patch reflected the problem of identifying men in a mass conscript or draft army. In time, the patch would become a focus for unit pride, which also has its reverse in ridicule for other divisional patches. The 82nd Airborne Division patch — a double 'A' for 'All American' — was read as 'Almost Airborne' by the men of the 101st Airborne. In turn the 82nd would ridicule the 'Screaming Eagle' of the 101st with references to 'Screaming Chickens'. Sometimes there was self deprecation, as when the 5th Special Forces Group in Vietnam referred to their patch as the 'Saigon Electrical Works'.

The 9th Infantry have a blue, red and white octofoil patch — the heraldic symbol of the ninth son. In Vietnam the patch was nicknamed 'Flower Power' or 'The Psychedelic Cookie' Division. In World War II men of the 90th Infantry Divison from Texas and Oklahoma asserted that the white letters 'TO', which resemble a rancher's brand, did not stand for the two states but for 'Tough Ombres' — Tough Guys. A number of the patches worn by US

Army Divisions in Europe in World War II reflected US participation in World War I: the 79th had a Cross of Lorraine and the 93rd the silhouette of a French helmet. Men of the 92nd had a Buffalo, which dated back to the Indian Wars of the Midwest, when black soldiers serving in what was traditionally a Negro division were known as 'Buffaloes' by the Indians.

After the Spanish-American War uniforms changed from blue to khaki. During World War II there was a move from khaki to olive drab and in the 1970s to camouflage colors. Throughout these transitions the principle behind unit patches remained the same. The backing material for patches and badges changed from khaki to olive drab in the 1960s. In the 1960s in Vietnam, and now privately in the United States, individual soldiers had badges embroidered directly onto their fatigue shirts and jackets.

■ CAREERS AND THE ■ 'MENU BOARD'

Rank, performance, skills or trades, length of service and unit are all displayed on different parts of a soldier's jacket or shirt. In the US Army, officers display rank on collars or epaulettes, NCOs on the upper sleeve or collar. The current unit in which a soldier is serving is worn on the left shoulder while the one in which he saw action is

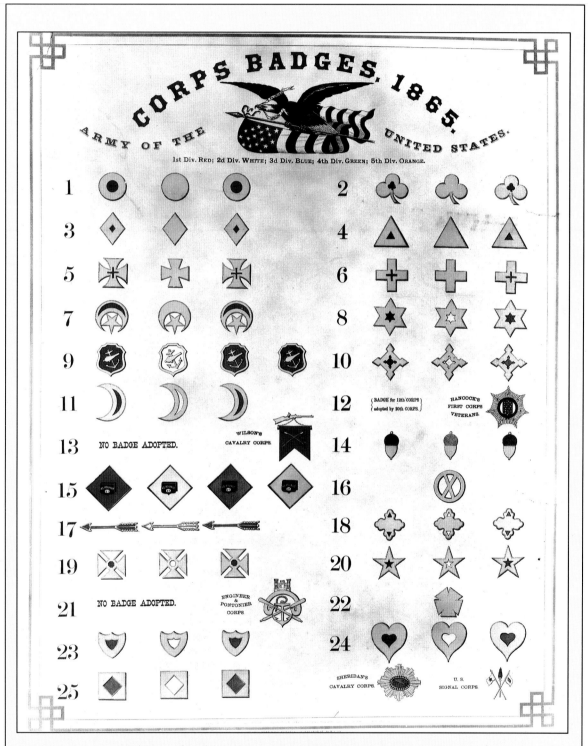

Corps badges first appeared in 1862 (on the Union side)
and were standardized by General Hooker the following
year, who assigned colors to the divisions within each
corps.

Lieutenant General Ulysses S. Grant at Cold Harbour Virginia in June 1864. The rank insignia on the shoulders is still perpetuated in US Army Dress Blue uniforms. The business-like uniform reflects the need for comfort in the field rather than the parade ground style of peace time armies.

worn on the right shoulder. Thus General Galvin, Supreme Allied Commander Europe, SACEUR, wears a 1st Cavalry patch on his right shoulder, since he served with 'the Cav' in Vietnam. Special trades or training are worn on or above shirt or jacket chest pockets. When a soldier is in dress greens with his medal ribbons, qualification and trade badges, divisional patch, rank, service stripes and name tag on his tunic he is sometimes described as wearing his 'menu board'. A knowledgable observer can read off the man's career and service simply by identifying ribbons, badges and patches.

Special skill badges include Parachutist, Senior Parachutist and Master Parachutist wings, Pathfinder, Air Assault, EOD (senior and master) Diver (in four classes) Scuba Diver and, perhaps rather chillingly, Basic Nuclear

Reactor Operator (2nd Class NRO, 1st Class NRO and NRO Shift Supervisor). Parachutists' wings are sometimes worn informally on the front of caps and combat hats, though rank is normally displayed here. One Advisor to Vietnamese forces in the early 1960s wore an entirely non-issue black French-style beret with his wings and the distinctive floral rank badges of a captain in the Army of the Republic of Vietnam (ARVN).

In dress greens, the branch of service insignia — for example, engineers, infantry, armor or chemical corps — are displayed in gold-colored metal on a circular backing for enlisted men. They appear in other colors and without the backing for officers and are worn by all ranks on lower lapels.

Airborne wings are second only in prestige to the Ranger tab. The word 'tab' distinguishes this narrow crescent-shaped cloth badge from larger unit patches. Distinctive in black and yellow, the Ranger tab is awarded to men who have completed the gruelling training course conducted in mountain, swamp and woodland scrub terrain. A three-tour Vietnam veteran told the author that he never experienced anything as tough as Ranger training, even when he was on active operations in Vietnam.

In the 1950s the US Army introduced name tags sewn above the right pocket of shirts and jackets, while on the opposite side, in yellow letters on black, were the words 'US Army'. These distinctions made sense in a world in which many NATO and Allied armies wore very similar uniforms. The name tag was also useful for quick identification of the soldier in the field. On dress greens and other formal wear the tag is a black plastic badge with white lettering. The Vietnam War saw the move to subdued insignia and cloth name tags, and badges became a mix of black and olive drab. Patches which had been a rainbow of colors were changed to a mix of black and olive drab, though some of the texture of the black embroidery did convey an idea of the original color and design. The transition also produced some odd mixes of uniforms, with full color divisional patches contrasting with subdued name and US Army tags and even some in-country modifications.

One veteran recalled to the author how his Special Forces A and B Teams could be distinguished in base camps. The men of the A Team, who were in contact with North Vietnamese and regular VietCong forces, wore highly colored South Vietnamese and US Army insignia, including a two-color cravat. Their B Team companions, who worked in the greater security of a base supply area, had the complete subdued olive drab insignia. An uninformed visitor would have assumed from

ABOVE A meeting of minds — General Galvin SACEUR
— Supreme Allied Commander Europe — receives a
briefing from a CBW clad officer. General Galvin wears
the 1st Cavalry patch on his right shoulder since he served
with the unit in combat in Vietnam.

TOP Pvt. Willy Edward and Milton Wainsright of Co. A, 2d
Bn, 30th Inf. 3 Div. on Exercise Marne Might in 1965. The
Div patch can just be seen on the jacket of the right hand man.

appearances that the roles were reversed.

In part this can be explained by the fact that rear areas are where dress and insignia discipline are enforced by officers and Military Police. In the rear, troops can also retain some control over the laundering and issue of their clothing. In the field, when bundles of fatigues arrive, men rarely bother with badges and patches.

As far back as World War II badges and patches were being collected. Today, there are both fakes and forgeries on the market, as well as simply modern patches which have been made by manufacturers and never issued. Knowledgable collectors can identify fakes by the degree of wear and fading, the materials used and the quality of workmanship. However, even modern badges can be 'distressed' to look like twenty- or thirty- or even fifty-year-old insignia. New or old, the color and design of US Army patches still exert a fascination, reflecting over 100 years of history and service.

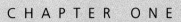

CHAPTER ONE

MAKING AND FAKING

Two officers — one a Ranger qualified soldier with the
82nd Airborne and the other a Major with the 101st with
Master Parachutist Wings discuss tactics during Exercise
Golden Pheasant in Honduras in March 1988

Over the years, US Army insignia has been produced using a variety of machine embroidery techniques. Some are very old and all have characteristic features. The first work was done in the United States in the late 1880s, on 107 class trade or Irish swing-needle machines, as they were popularly known. Domestic machines were also used and these techniques are still employed by Third World embroiderers with great skill and artistry.

From World War II to the late 1950s, the US Army wore tunics and jackets in a color generally called khaki. Correctly, it was Olive Drab Shade No 33 or No 51, and there was a lighter color Khaki, Army Shade No 1. Shoulder patches from this period have either a narrow tan or pale khaki edge, or no visible edge at all.

In 1957 the introduction of new Army Green Uniform saw the move to patches with a dark green edge. By the mid-1960s the characteristic feature of machine-made badges was the merrowed edge. This is a solid band of chain stitching which stands proud of the badge and which ends in a 'tail' of thread which is normally stuck to the back of the badge. The edge helps to protect the material and prevent fraying.

Clearly then, a World War II badge which has a merrowed edge is a modern copy. The problem with copies and fakes is where badges are produced locally by small-scale operations. During World War II the British produced equipment and clothing as well as badges for the US Army. Singer machines which could produce variable satin stitches and straight filling stitches were used. Some overseas copies of US badges are recognizable by the use of colored cloth in the construction of the badge to save thread. In early designs this was with felts, but in the Far East silks have since found favor.

Patches produced for US servicemen in Korea, Vietnam, Thailand and the Philippines have a unique charm of their own. As a rough guide, the Thai-made patches are the finest, using small panels of matched silk to make up the background colors. The least well finished are the Vietnamese-made — they were often put together on a domestic sewing machine — the problem with this is that finer detail must be done by hand. Interestingly, examples of Vietnamese badges exist in a plastic wallet with a button tag, so that they can be hung from a shirt pocket in the French style. Conventional sewing machine-made patches require the embroiderer to move the fabric so that it is oversewed many times with ordinary stitches. The Vietnamese-made patches sewn in this way are therefore rather crude. The method is unsuitable when fine detail or a heavier weight of work is required.

Philippine patches are better made and continue to be produced. One experienced American collector explained

198th Inf Brigade (subdued) – black embroidered thread on an OD cloth patch, normally the black background is also embroidered)

32nd Arty Brigade

44th Medical Brigade

22nd Signal Brigade (subdued, the mechanical embroidery on this patch has been incorrectly programmed and the motif is off center).

18th Medical Brigade

The Imjin Scouts patch on a fatigue shirt of an unnamed Spec 4 in the 2nd Infantry Division.

that he had a contact in Manilla who could make a perfect copy of any badge you could name. Valuable and rare privately-made Vietnam era badges could therefore be faked. Ageing can be achieved by an overnight soaking in coffee or a dilute soft drink and a little distressing. Stone-washed designer jeans get much the same treatment.

The Japanese and Taiwanese also produced patches and insignia during the Vietnam War and their quality is superior to any Far Eastern work. Many modern 'fun' patches are made in Taiwan.

The only way a fake patch handmade in the Far East can be identified with certainty is to examine its origins and likely availability. Where only a few hundred were produced and worn in Vietnam or Korea the chances of a real badge coming onto the market are rare.

The real problem arises with World War II, Korean or Vietnam War patches which are collectable if they are locally made. A good modern handmade copy looks like the real thing. Pakistan has an internationally-respected reputation for its gold and silver thread work — World War II badges like the China, India and Burma 'Flying Tigers' can be faked and are so collectable and attractive that they still command good prices.

When there is no pretence at faking, many veterans are proud to wear a top-quality gold and silver thread version of their divisional patch on a blazer or jacket.

Where patches have been unstitched from a shirt or jacket the threads often remain. Though these could be faked, this is a relatively reliable and quick way of checking if the badge is authentic and has been worn on clothing. Many patches are manufactured, but never issued, and though they are good representations of insignia, they went straight from the workshop to the dealer, never stopping on a uniform en route.

Another quick check is the starch and wear on the badge. Since many have been worn on fatigue shirts the starch has entered the fabric, and they may even retain the crease from the sleeve. In addition, the effects of sunshine and rain will bleach out the color in a patch that has seen service. Locally made insignia from Vietnam are particularly prone to fading.

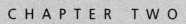

CHAPTER TWO

THE FAMILY TREE

In a classic World War II 'action' picture Doughboys
pose with infantry weapons. The man on the left with the
M1 Garand appears to have the 80th Division patch
showing the Blue Ridge Mountains on the shoulder of his
combat jacket.

US Army Engineers of the first contingent of soldiers to arrive in Glasgow, Scotland in 1917 stand with their rifles and canteens piled. The soldiers have no distinguishing features except their metal collar insignia and the cords on their campaign hats.

The structure of the US Army is rather like that of a family tree. Divided into Army units with their own area of operation and their own history and traditions, further subdivisions of Corps and Divisions follow. Each has its patch which reflects its special identity.

During World War I, some units were activated, but did not actually serve overseas. Those that did see action in France collected battle honors and insignia which reflected their service. World War II saw involvement on a larger scale and in different theaters of war. The unit patch, embroidered in silk, became a focus for pride as US Army and Air Force units mingled with Allied forces in North Africa and, toward the end of the War, in Italy and Northern Europe. In the Pacific the US Marine Corps and the US Army island-hopped toward Japan, and there was less contact with Allies. At the end of the War, some of these units were disbanded, and their patches have become collector's items. However, as the survey of Divisions below shows, many remain part of the Active Army, while others form part of the Army Reserve or the National Guard.

∎ ARMY PATCHES ∎

The army units are the top tier of the structure of the US armed forces. Their patches often reveal the influence of history. In the 1930s, the 1st Army's patch was an 'A' on a ground colored according to the branch of service of the wearer in the upper half of the patch. This was later simplified to a red and white ground.

The 2nd Army patch features a red and white '2' on a khaki ground. The 3rd Army has the letters 'A' and 'O', the latter commemorating the fact that it was the army of occupation in Germany in 1918. The 4th Army patch has a white four-leaf clover on red ground.

Soldiers of the 2nd Infantry Division climb the bluffs above Omaha Beach in Normandy. The Indian Head patch is clearly visible on their combat jackets.

The original form of the 5th Army's patch was five stars, but this was changed to feature a silhouette of a mosque, commemorating its organization at Oujda, Morocco, in January 1943. The new patch was officially approved by General Mark W. Clark.

Early versions of the 6th Army's patch were a simple six-pointed star. Later, the letter 'A' was added. A red triangle with seven yellow steps on either side is the patch of the 7th Army, while the 8th Army has a white cross on red. The 9th Army patch has an 'A' within a petal-shaped border on a red ground.

Not shown here are the patches of the 10th Army (an 'X' formed as two triangles), and the 15th Army (an 'A' on a five-sided shape with red and white blocks forming a roman 'X'). The 14th Army was a 'ghost unit' which existed on paper only.

■ CORPS PATCHES ■

As with Army patches, the Corps patches during World War II reflect unit identity and history. A description of each follows:

1ST CORPS

A white circle on a black field.

2ND CORPS

A 'II' flanked by the American Eagle and British Lion. 2nd Corps landed in North Africa, and with the 4th, 6th and 21st subsequently fought in Italy.

1st Army (new)

2nd Army

3rd Army

4th Army

5th Army (new)

6th Army

7th Army

8th Army

OD service jacket used by a medical corps Sergeant on demobilization after World War II. The meritorious service insignia is displayed on the right forearm and the discharge insignia is above the right breast pocket.

General Mark W Clark in an open air HQ in Italy. The 5th Army patch is just visible on his shoulder and his general's stars on shirt collar and overseas cap. The WAC with the telephone has the chevrons of a Technician 4th Grade.

3RD CORPS

A caltrop insignia in blue with black border (a caltrop is a spiked device used to hobble horses or pierce pneumatic tires). 3rd Corps is nicknamed 'Phantom Corps' following its surprise attacks on German forces in the Ardennes in 1944-45. Today, 3rd Corps is the Reforger force for rapid reinforcement of NATO in Europe.

4TH CORPS

A circle divided in four blue and white segments.

5TH CORPS

A five-sided blue patch with white edges.

6TH CORPS

A '6' on a blue circle.

7TH CORPS

Originally a '7' on a six-pointed shield, but this was changed to a 'VII' on a red seven-pointed star.

8TH CORPS

An '8' on a blue field.

9TH CORPS

A red 'IX' on a blue field.

10TH CORPS

A 'X' on a blue and white field.

11TH CORPS

Originally a heraldic shield, changed to two dice showing the score of 11.

12TH CORPS

A windmill representing New Amsterdam (New York).

13TH CORPS

To avoid the unlucky associations of the number, a green four-leaf clover and red triangle was adopted.

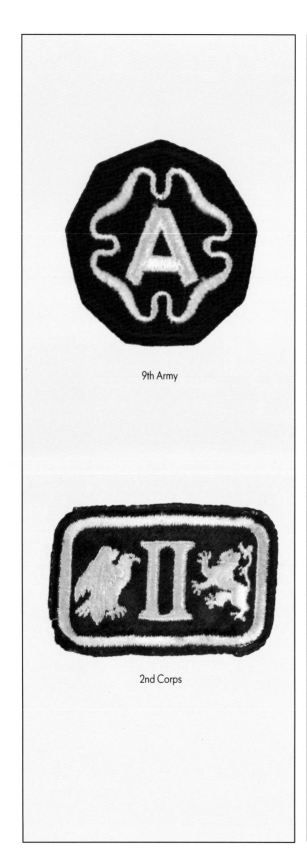

9th Army

2nd Corps

Radio operators of Co B, 503rd Inf Battle Group, 82nd Airborne Division during a live firing exercise 'Sunshade IV' at Fort Bragg in January 1963. They have full color insignia and characteristic airborne boots and pants.

14TH CORPS

A blue 'X' and a red four-pointed star.

15TH CORPS

Originally a blue and white 'XV', but this was changed to a more original design with the 'X' superimposed upon the 'V'.

16TH CORPS

A shield with a blue border enclosing a four pointed star. The star is surrounded by a white serrated circle.

17TH CORPS

Interestingly there is no evidence of a patch for the 17th Corps. It does not even appear to have been a 'ghost' unit.

18TH CORPS

Originally a blue dragon's head set at an angle on a diamond-shaped field. When the 18th became an Airborne corps, the Airborne tab was placed square above, with the dragon looking down to the left.

19TH CORPS

Originally the Liberty Bell in red with yellow border. This was changed to a white tomahawk on a blue, white-bordered circle.

20TH CORPS

Two yellow interlocked 'X's on a shield.

3rd Corps

5th Corps

8th Corps

10th Corps

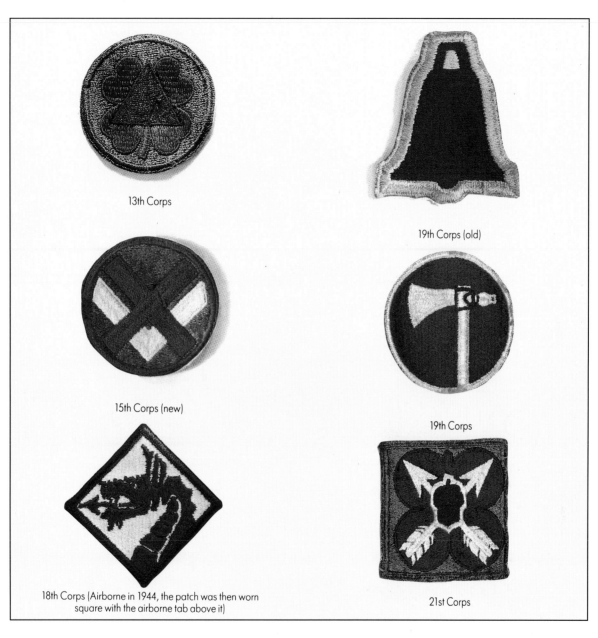

13th Corps

19th Corps (old)

15th Corps (new)

19th Corps

18th Corps (Airborne in 1944, the patch was then worn square with the airborne tab above it)

21st Corps

OPPOSITE Anonymous in British snow camouflage overalls a 81mm mortar M1 crew prepare to fire on a German position near St Vith, Belgium, 1944.

21ST CORPS
A red acorn pierced by two arrows.

22ND CORPS
An arrowhead.

23RD CORPS
Three crossed arrows.

24TH CORPS
A heart, the insignia first adopted by the 24th during the Civil War.

36TH CORPS
A blue patch with an interlocked '3' and '6', plus a red and white three-pointed star interlocked with a smaller star.

The 31st and 33rd Corps were 'ghost units', which existed on paper only during World War II.

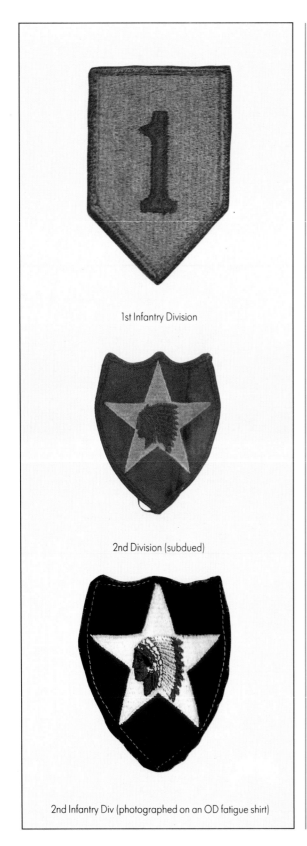

1st Infantry Division

2nd Division (subdued)

2nd Infantry Div (photographed on an OD fatigue shirt)

■ DIVISIONAL PATCHES ■

Divisonal patches are perhaps the best known of all the insignia in the US Army. Being smaller units, the divisions became the focus of the serving soldier's loyalty and pride, and many divisions have nicknames and mottoes, giving them a particular individual identity. The divisional patches were worn in both World Wars, and many divisions also saw service in Korea and in Vietnam during the post-World War II period. A brief description of each Division's insignia and history is given below:

1ST INFANTRY DIVISION

'The Big Red One', originally formed as the First Expeditionary Division in World War I. In World War II it fought Rommel's Afrika Corps in North Africa, and was also operational in Sicily. It landed at Omaha Beach and advanced with the Allies into Germany. 1st Inf. Div. served a total of 1,656 days in Vietnam. It is an Active Army Division based at Fort Riley, Kansas, and at Goppingen, West Germany.

2ND INF. DIV.

With its 'Indian Head' patch, 2nd Inf. Div. saw action in both World Wars. In World War II it fought in Normandy, the Ardennes and in Czechoslovakia, and later saw action in Korea. It is an Active Army Division, based at Camp Casey, Republic of South Korea.

3RD INF. DIV.

The 'Marne', an honor earned during their service in World War I. The patch is three white bars on a blue background, which is the Infantry color. The narrow border is all that remains of an original Khaki ground. In World War II, the Marne saw action in Sicily, Cassino, Anzio, the Colmar Pocket and Munich. It also served in the Korean War. An Active Army Division, it is based at Wurzburg, West Germany.

4TH INF. DIV.

The 'Ivy Division', with a khaki diamond-shaped patch containing a green four-pronged, four-leafed ivy. Originally, the patch was tombstone-shaped. The 4th fought in France in both World Wars, and was the first US Division to enter Paris in 1944, and later, to reach German soil. It served a total of 1,534 days in Vietnam and is based at Fort Carson, Colorado.

5TH INF. DIV.

The 'Red Diamond' Division fought in both World Wars, and its 1st Brigade served in Vietnam between 1968 and

1971. It is Active Army Division with Reserve elements, based at Fort Polk, Louisiana.

GIs with a 60mm mortar M2 in World War II. The censor has painted out the insignia on their helmets.

6TH INF. DIV.

During World War I the 6th 'Sight-seeing' Inf. Div. patch was a small red six-pointed star with a '6' in center. The number has since gone and the star grown larger. The 6th served in New Guinea and the Philippines in World War II. It is an Active Army Division with Reserve and National Guard elements, based at Fort Richardson, Arkansas.

7TH INF. DIV.

The 'Hourglass' patch is formed by two crossed '7's, one of which is inverted. The 7th served in both World Wars and also in Korea. It is an Active Army Division, based at Fort Ord, California.

8TH INF. DIV.

The patch has an '8' pierced by a Golden Arrow. It served in both World Wars and received its nickname of 'Pathfinder Division' serving in Brittany, Duren and Cologne during World War II. An Active Army Division, it is based at Bad Kreuznach, West Germany.

9th INF. DIV.

The 'Old Reliables', or 'Varsity' were constituted on August 1, 1940, at Fort Bragg, and subsequently served in North Africa, Sicily, the Cotentin Peninsula and Germany. 3rd Brigade was part of the Riverine Force in Vietnam and served 985 days. Its insignia is a nine-petaled flower in red and blue. The 9th is an Active Division, with National Guard elements, based at Fort Lewis.

Paratroops of the 101st struggle with a crashed glider after landings in Holland in September 1944. The censor has scratched out the Screaming Eagle patch on the combat jackets and helmets, but their Stars and Stripes arm bands and patches are clearly visible.

10TH INF. DIV.

In World War I, the patch was an 'X' within a circle. During World War II, the Division trained for mountain operations and adopted crossed bayonets, and had the tab 'Mountain' above, which earned the nickname of 'Mountaineers'. It served on the Gothic Line and the Po Valley. An Active Division with National Guard elements, it is based at Fort Drum, New York State.

11TH INF. DIV.

11th became an Airborne Division in World War II, and adopted a new patch with Airborne tab and a winged '11' inside a shield, and gained the nickname 'Angels'. In World War II, the 11th served at Leyte, Manilla and Cavite.

12TH INF. DIV.

In World War I, the 12th had a diamond-shaped patch containing a bayonet, two stars and the figure '12'. By World War II this had changed to a yellow steer's head on a red shield. Action in the Pacific earned the nickname of 'Philippine'.

13TH INF. DIV.

The 13th's World War I insignia featured a '13' within a lucky horseshoe and a black cat. On becoming Airborne in World War II it adopted a winged unicorn inside a shield and Airborne tab. The Division served in Europe.

14TH INF. DIV.

Formed in World War I and called the Wolverine Division, the patch featured a silhouette of a wolverine within a shield.

17TH INF. DIV.

'Thunder from Heaven'. The patch features an eagle's claw within a circle and an Airborne tab. The Division participated in the Rhine crossings in 1945.

18TH INF. DIV.

'Cactus' Division — the patch features an '18' within a

3rd Infantry Div

4th Infantry Div

5th Infantry Div

6th Infantry Div

7th Infantry Div

8th Infantry Div

8th Inf Div (subdued)
Actual size same as 23rd Div bottom right

9th Infantry Div

10th Infantry Div (trained for mountain warfare, the
Division later wore a Mountain tab above its patch)

11th Airborne Div

17th Airborne Div

23rd (Americal) Div

Men of the 4th Infantry Division shelter behind the sea
wall at Utah beach during the landings at Normandy in
June 1944. The censor has obscured the patches for
security reasons, but the diamond shape is just visible.

clump of cacti and the motto: *Noli Me Tangere* (Do not touch me). The Division was formed in World War I.

19TH INF. DIV.

Another World War I formation. The patch shows a 'G' within a circle and inverted triangle.

23RD INF. DIV.

The 'Americal'. Its patch shows the stars of the Southern Cross on a blue shield. In World War II, the Americal served in Guadalcanal, Bougainville and Cebu Island, and became part of the occupation force in Japan. In Vietnam, it was described as: 'the Army's only named Division on active service'.

24TH INF. DIV.

The 'Victory' Division's patch shows a green taro leaf (a common tropical plant) against a red circle. In World War II it saw action in New Guinea and the Philippines, and later fought in Korea. An Active Army Division, with National Guard elements, it is based at Fort Stewart, California.

25TH INF. DIV.

A red taro leaf with a bolt of lightning — hence its name, 'Tropic Lightning'. The Division was formed in Hawaii in 1941 and was at Pearl Harbor when the Japanese attacked. Later in World War II it served in Guadalcanal, New Georgia and the Philippines. It also saw action during the Korean and Vietnam Wars. An Active Army Division, the 25th is based at Schofield Barracks, Hawaii.

26TH INF. DIV.

The 'Yankees'. Their patch has the letters 'Y' and 'D' as a monogram cattle-brand on a khaki diamond. It served in Europe in World War I and fought in the Battle of the Bulge in World War II. It is now part of the National Guard and is based at Boston, Massachusetts.

27TH INF. DIV.

The 'New York' has a brand-style monogram 'NY' in red

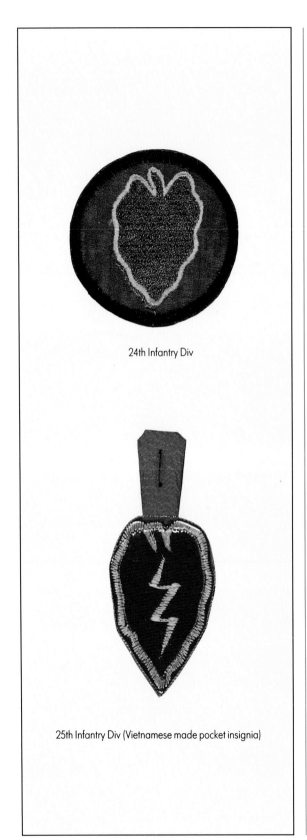

24th Infantry Div

25th Infantry Div (Vietnamese made pocket insignia)

on a black field. In World War I it incorporated the constellation of Orion on its patch as a pun on its commander's name — Maj. Gen. J. F. O'Ryan. During World War II, the 27th fought in the Makin Islands, Saipan and Okinawa.

▨▨▨▨▨ 28TH INF. DIV. ▨▨▨▨▨

The 'Keystone' is the red keystone of the State Seal of Pennsylvania, and had the alternative name of 'the bucket of blood'. As well as service during World War I, the 29th was in on the liberation of Paris and the fighting in Hurtgen Forest and the Colmar Pocket in World War II. It is now part of the National Guard, and is based at Harrisburg, Pennsylvania.

▨▨▨▨▨ 29TH INF. DIV. ▨▨▨▨▨

The 29th incorporated the blue and gray colors of the two sides in the Civil War into a Ying-Yang symbol. It fought in both World Wars and is now part of the National Guard, based at Fort Belvoir, Virginia.

▨▨▨▨▨ 30TH INF. DIV. ▨▨▨▨▨

'Old Hickory' — a patch with 'XXX' within an 'H', which is in turn encompassed by the letter 'O'. The 30th saw service in World War I and fought at St Lo, Aachen, Malmedy, Stavelot and in the Rhine crossings in World War II.

▨▨▨▨▨ 31ST INF. DIV. ▨▨▨▨▨

The 'Dixie Division' has two back-to-back 'D's on its patch. It fought in World War I and in the Philippines in World War II.

▨▨▨▨▨ 32ND INF. DIV. ▨▨▨▨▨

The 'Red Arrow' originally had its red arrow with a bar on a khaki ground, but this was later removed to produce an austere Divisional patch. Active in World War I, the 32nd also fought in the Pacific in World War II.

▨▨▨▨▨ 33RD INF. DIV. ▨▨▨▨▨

Known as the 'Prairie', the patch is a yellow cross against a black circle. The Division fought in World War I and in northern Luzon, in the Philippines, in World War II.

▨▨▨▨▨ 34TH INF. DIV. ▨▨▨▨▨

Nicknamed the 'Red Bull', the 34th had the motto 'Sandstorm Division' in World War I, and the patch had a red bull's skull and the number '34'. In World War II this had been simplified to the skull on a black background shaped like the Mexican *olla*, or flask. The Division fought in Tunisia, Cassino, the Gothic Line and the Po Valley.

35TH INF. DIV.

The 'Santa Fe' adopted the cross symbol used to mark the Santa Fe trail. It fought in Europe in both World Wars and is currently part of the National Guard, based at Fort Leavenworth, Kansas.

36TH INF. DIV.

The 'Texas' patch has a khaki 'T' inside a blue-gray shape resembling a flint arrowhead. The 36th fought in World War I and at Salerno, Cassino and in France and Germany during World War II.

37TH INF. DIV.

An Ohio Division with a patch of a red circle within a white border, earning the nickname of 'Buckeye'. It fought in World War I and at Munda, Bougainville, Lingayen Gulf and Manilla in World War II.

38TH INF. DIV.

Known as 'Cyclone Division'. The patch has the letters 'C' and 'Y' within a blue and red shield. It fought in World War I and at Bataan in World War II.

39TH INF. DIV.

'Delta Division' fought in World War I, but did not go overseas in World War II. Its original patch was a circle with a triangle enclosing three smaller triangles in red, white and blue, symbolizing the three states of the Mississsipi delta: Mississipi, Louisiana and Arkansas. The patch was simplified to a red triangle enclosing the letter 'D'.

40TH INF. DIV.

The 'Sunburst Division' — its patch has a gold sun on a blue diamond. It fought in both World Wars and in Korea. It is currently part of the US Army Reserve and National Guard, based at Los Alamitos, California.

41ST INF. DIV.

'Sunset' or the 'Jungleers' — a semi-circular patch showing a Pacific Ocean sunset. The Division fought in World War I and at Salamaua, the Marshall Islands, Mindanao and Palawan in World War II.

42ND INF. DIV.

The 42nd 'Rainbow' Division fought in World War I and at Schweinfurt and Munich in World War II, when it also liberated Dachau.

43RD INF. DIV.

Known as 'Red Wing', or 'Winged Victory', the 43rd has

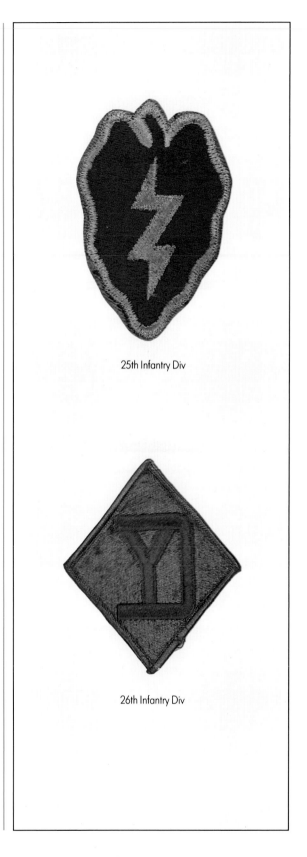

25th Infantry Div

26th Infantry Div

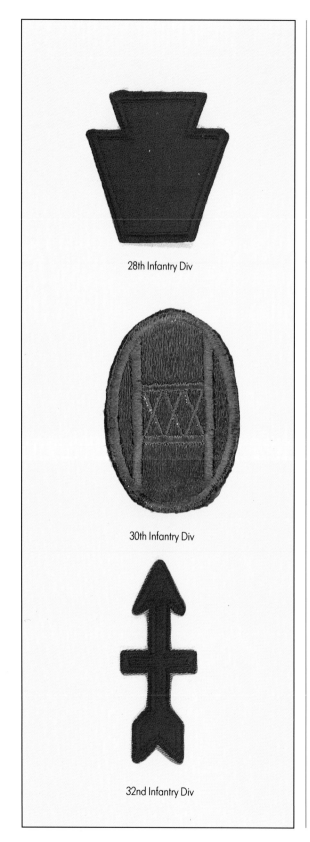

28th Infantry Div

30th Infantry Div

32nd Infantry Div

a patch with a black grape leaf on a red background, symbolizing the four states of New England. The 43rd fought in New Georgia, New Guinea and Luzon in World War II.

44TH INF. DIV.

The patch has two blue figure '4's back-to-back, forming an arrowhead on a yellow background. It served in the Saar, Ulm and Danube rivers during World War II.

45TH INF. DIV.

A yellow Indian thunderbird on a red diamond gives the unit its nickname. An earlier patch had a yellow swastika — insignia hardly suitable during World War II, where it saw action at Salerno, Cassino and the Belfort Gap. It also served in Korea. The patch is still worn by the 45th Infantry Brigade (Separate) of the Oklahoma Army National Guard, which replaced the Division in 1968.

46TH INF. DIV.

Although assigned two patches, this was a 'ghost unit' in World War II.

47TH INF. DIV.

The patch features a Viking helmet — the Division was reputed to have a large number of Norwegian Americans. It is part of the National Guard, based at St Paul, Minnesota.

48TH INF. DIV.

Another 'ghost' division.

49TH INF. DIV.

The patch features a gold-panner on a red and yellow shield.

50TH INF. DIV.

A 'ghost' division.

51ST INF. DIV.

A yellow and blue five-sided patch with a rattlesnake motif.

55TH INF. DIV.

A 'ghost' division.

59TH INF. DIV.

A 'ghost' division.

63RD INF. DIV.

'Blood and Fire' — the 63rd has a red, drop-shaped

33rd Infantry Div

34th Infantry Div

39th Infantry Div

40th Infantry Div

41st Infantry Div

46th Division

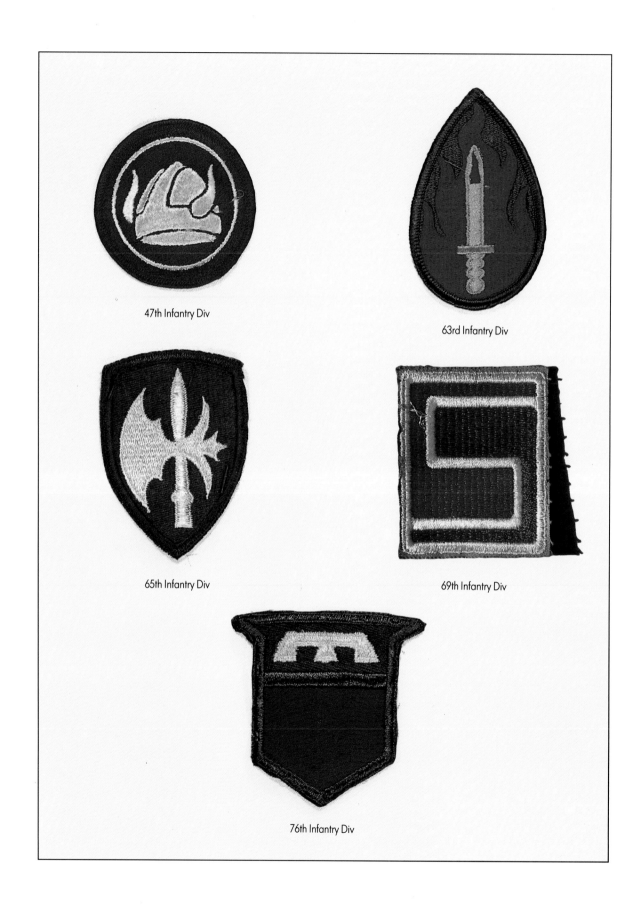

47th Infantry Div

63rd Infantry Div

65th Infantry Div

69th Infantry Div

76th Infantry Div

patch terminating in fire, enclosing a yellow bayonet with a drop of blood on the tip. It fought in Bavaria and on the Danube during World War II.

65TH INF. DIV.

The patch features a white halberd within a blue shield — hence the name 'Battle-Axe'. It fought in Saarlautern, Regensburg and on the Danube during World War II.

66TH INF. DIV.

During World War I, the 66th had a circular patch showing a black panther. In World War II this was changed to a snarling panther's head. It may have been thought that the first patch looked too much like a domestic cat, or that it was too similar to the patch of the 81st Division (see illustration on page 38). The 66th bottled up German forces at St Nazaire and Lorient during World War II.

69TH INF. DIV.

The 'Fighting Sixty-Ninth' has the figures '6' and '9' interlocked in blue and red. It saw action in Germany during World War II.

70TH INF. DIV.

The 'Trailblazers' have a rather quaint patch showing a white woodsman's axe with a green tree and white mountain in the background, all on a red field. The Division served at Saarbrucken and on the Moselle River during World War II.

71ST INF. DIV.

'The Red Circle' — a circular white patch, bordered in red, containing the figures '7' and '1' set at an angle. The 71st served in southern Germany in World War II.

75TH INF. DIV.

The 75th's patch has a '7' and '5' against a red, white and blue shield. The Division served in the Ardennes and Westphalia in World War II.

76TH INF. DIV.

The 'Liberty Bell' — the shield-shaped patch is red in the lower half and blue at the top with white motif. It saw action in World War I and in Luxembourg and Germany in World War II.

77TH INF. DIV.

The Division of New York State, the 'Statue of Liberty' patch has the statue in yellow outline. It fought in World War I and in Guam, Leyte and Okinawa in World War II.

GIs on the way to Normandy wear a khaki sleeve over their Divisional Patches. This simple security precaution would prevent identification of the unit when it embarked or disembarked and would save the censor the task of erasing the insignia from photographs.

78TH INF. DIV.

The 'Lightning' Division — the patch features a white lightning bolt on a red semi-circle. It fought in World War I and at Aachen and the Roer and Ruhr rivers in World War II.

79TH INF. DIV.

'Lorraine' — a white Cross of Lorraine on a blue shield. The patch commemorates the Division's service in France in World War I. It returned to France in World War II, seeing action in the Vosges and in Normandy.

80TH INF. DIV.

The 'Blue Ridge' Division's patch in World War I showed blue ridges with the motto: 'Vis Montium', and the figure '80'. In World War II, when the Division fought in Normandy, the Moselle and at the Relief of Bastogne, the patch was simplified to show just three ridges, representing the three States of Pennsylvania, Virginia and West Virginia.

77th Infantry Div

81st Infantry Div

81ST INF. DIV.

The 'Wild Cat' — the patch shows a black, stub-tailed cat against a khaki background. The Division fought in World War I and at Angaur, Peleliu and Ulithi in World War II.

82ND INF. DIV.

The 'All American' Division added its Airborne tab in World War II, where it fought in Sicily, Normandy and the Ardennes. It earned the nickname 'Baggypants' after a German officer had described 82nd Division paratroopers as 'devils in baggy pants'. Its 3rd Brigade saw service in Vietnam, and it is currently an Active Army unit based at Fort Bragg, North Carolina.

83RD INF. DIV.

The 'Ohio' or 'Thunderbolt' Division. The patch has a yellow monogram reading 'OHIO' on a black triangle. The Division fought in World War I and in Italy and Germany in World War II.

84TH INF. DIV.

In World War I, the 'Railsplitters' had a circular patch with an axe head and the number '84' surmounted with the name of 'Lincoln'. In World War II — where they fought in Ardennes and at Hanover — the patch was simplified to a white axe splitting a rail.

85TH INF. DIV.

The 'Custer Division' patch had the letters 'C' and 'D' in red on a khaki circle. The 85th fought in World War I and in Italy in World War II.

86TH INF. DIV.

The 'Black Hawk' Division patch has a red shield with a black hawk, with a smaller shield bearing the letters 'BH'. It saw service in World War I and fought in southern Germany and liberated Dachau in World War II.

87TH INF. DIV.

The patch has a yellow acorn on a green circle — hence the name 'Golden Acorn'. The Division served in both World Wars, seeing action in the Ardennes, Germany and on the Czech border in World War II.

88TH INF. DIV.

Known as the 'Cloverleaf', the patch features two figure '8's combined to make a clover-leaf shape. However, the Division preferred to adopt the name 'Blue Devil'. In World War II it saw action in northern Italy.

89TH INF. DIV.

The patch has an 'M' within a circle which, when inverted becomes a 'W' — hence the name 'Rolling W', standing for Middle West. It fought in World War I and at Bingen, Eisenach and central Germany in World War II.

82nd Airborne Div

86th Infantry Div

90th Infantry Div

82nd Airborne Div (subdued)

88th Infantry Div

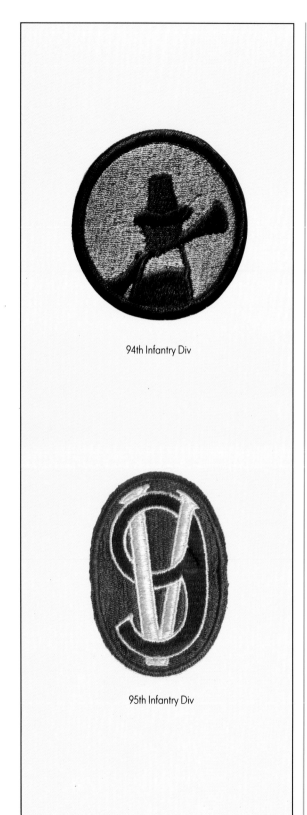

94th Infantry Div

95th Infantry Div

90TH INF. DIV.

The 'Tough Ombres' mentioned in the introduction. The 90th fought in World War I and saw action in Normandy, Metz and Czechoslovakia in World War II.

91ST INF. DIV.

The 'Wild West' patch features a green fir tree. The Division fought in both World Wars, seeing action in Italy during World War II.

92ND INF. DIV.

The 'Buffaloes' — a black buffalo on a khaki patch dates back to the Indian Wars of the last century. They served in both World Wars.

93RD INF. DIV.

The 93rd's patch reflects their service in World War I, when they were assigned to the French Army. It features a French World War I helmet in green on a black ground. The 93rd saw action in the Pacific in World War II.

94TH INF. DIV.

The earlier 94th patch showed a New Englander with a blunderbus on his shoulder. This was changed to a more prosaic circular patch with '9' and '4' in khaki and black during World War II, when the Division served in Brittany, the Siegrfried Line, the Saar and the Moselle River.

95TH INF. DIV.

Originally, the patch showed a K-shaped design within an oval. This was replaced by a red '9' with a white 'V' interlaced within an oval. The 'Victory' Division served at Metz, the Moselle River, the Siegfried Line and the Saar during World War II.

96th INF. DIV.

The 'Deadeye' Division had interlocked white and blue diamonds on a khaki background. It served in the Pacific during World War II.

97TH INF. DIV.

The patch was a white trident on a blue shield, hence the name 'Trident'. It served in central Germany in World War II.

98TH INF. DIV.

The 'Iroquois' patch was a shield in the colors of New Amsterdam with the head of an Iroquois indian in the center. It saw action in the Pacific during World War II.

99TH INF. DIV.

The patch is a black shield with a blue and white checkered band. The 'Checkerboard' served in the Ardennes and was at the Remagen bridgehead during World War II.

100TH INF. DIV.

The 'Century' patch has the number '100' in white and yellow on a blue shield. It served at Bitche, the Remagen bridgehead and the Saar during World War II.

101ST INF. DIV.

The 'Screaming Eagle' is, in fact, Old Abe, the mascot of the Iron Brigade in the American Civil War — the black shield of the patch also commemorates the Iron Brigade. The Division became Airborne in 1943, and served in Normandy and at Bastogne. The Division was committed to Vietnam in 1967 and served a total of 1,573 days. When subdued olive drab and black insignia were introduced in Vietnam, the Division, proud of its Screaming Eagle, retained the patch in full color. It is now an Active Airmobile helicopter-borne Division, based at Fort Cambell, Kentucky, and Fort Rucker, Alabama.

102ND INF. DIV.

The patch has the letter 'O' circling a 'Z', standing for the Ozark Mountains. The Division served on the Siegfried line and at the Ruhr and Munchen-Gladbach in World War II.

103RD INF. DIV.

The 'Cactus' Division. The patch shows a green cactus against a yellow circle. It served at Stuttgart and in Austria in World War II.

104TH INF. DIV.

The 'Timber Wolf' — the patch features a gray timber wolf's head against a green circle. The Division was prominent during the Rhine crossing at Cologne and the Ruhr in World War II.

106TH INF. DIV.

The 'Golden Lion' — a lion's head on a blue circle edged with white and red. The Division served at St Vith and in the Ardennes during World War II.

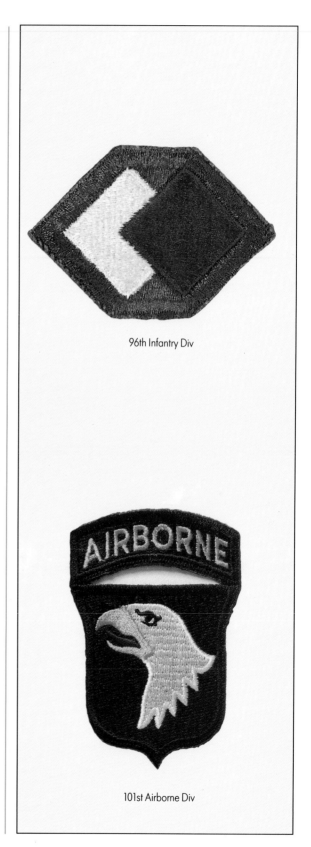

96th Infantry Div

101st Airborne Div

CHAPTER THREE

OTHER PATCHES:
CAVALRY, ARMORED DIVISION
AND BRIGADE PATCHES

A UH-1B Huey of the 1st Cavalry (Air Cav) lifts off from a
jungle LZ during operations in South Vietnam. The 1st
Cavalry were a pioneer force in airmobile operations
during the Vietnam War.

The patches of US Cavalry preserve the traditional yellow which first appeared in bandanas and piping on uniforms.

The 1st Cavalry — the 'First Team' or 'Hell for Leather' — saw action in the Philippines and was the first division to enter Tokyo. It served in Korea and was the first unit to enter Pyongyang in 1950. In Vietnam, it became an Air-mobile division and was credited with 2,056 days overseas and participated in many of the major operations.

It was reorganized into an armored division in 1975 and is currently an Active Army and Army National Guard Division, based at Fort Hood, Texas.

The 2nd Cavalry Division, like the 3rd, 21st, 24th, 56th, 61st, 62nd, 63rd, 64th, 65th and 66th, did not see action in World War II.

The 2nd and 3rd Cav., like 1st Cav., have yellow shield patches measuring 14×10 cm. The patches were said to have been designed by an officer's wife at Fort Bliss to be big enough to be visible through the dust kicked up by horse-mounted cavalry.

The 1st Cavalry's yellow shield has an oblique black bar and outline of a horse's head. The 2nd Cav.'s patch has a blue chevron and two stars, while 3rd Cav. have one with the figure '3' in blue. The 21st and 24th Cav. have the outline of a stirrup, while the 56th have a star. The 61st has a horse's head within a spur on a yellow shield, the 62nd a shield with crossed yellow bars and the 63rd a yellow square with crossed red bars. The 64th Cav.'s patch shows a saber on a yellow field, and the 65th's an arrowhead on a blue and yellow shield. The 66th has a six-pointed yellow star with a blue border.

∎ BRIGADE PATCHES ∎

A common, but not universal feature of US Army Brigade patches is the four-sided shape with a slight convex bulge at the top and bottom. For many National Guard

Armored Forces Headquarters

1st Armored Div

HELL ON WHEELS

2nd Armored Div

Brigades there is a strong State loyalty, and so the introduction of patches which reflected this was important for morale — particularly in the social climate of the 1960s.

Exceptions to the four-sided Brigade patches include shields, diamonds and circles. Some National Guard and Active Army Brigades were authorized in the 1960s to wear the World War II Divisional patch which corresponds to their number, thus perpetuating the memory of several famous Divisions. Examples of this include the 32nd Inf. Brigade which has the red arrow of the 32nd Infantry Div., the 33rd Inf. Brigade which has the yellow cross on a black circle of the 38th Inf. Div., the 40th Inf. Brigade with the gold sun on a blue diamond of the 40th Inf. Div., the 45th Inf. Brigade which has the Thunderbird of the 45th Inf. Div., though the 71st Airborne Bde., which is part of the Texas National Guard, has the insignia of the 36th Inf. Div.

Arm colors distinguish many brigade patches. So, for example, infantry have a predominantly blue design; artillery, red; medical, purple and military police, green. Artillery Brigades have arrows, cannon and missiles in yellow on a red field. Signals have lightning bolts, while logistics and transportation brigades have variations on yellow wheels against a brown field. Engineer units favor the castle of the Corps of Engineers and Civil Affairs have variants of a sword and pen or the torch of learning on blue.

One observer has noted the mixed heraldic origins of US Army Divisional and Brigade patches. Some draw on German and European designs and others on the shapes of native American patchworking traditions from the 19th century. Others, like the 81st Inf. Brigade, use designs borrowed from Red Indian totem poles. Some Hawaiian National Guard units have designs which look similar to the Japanese clan *mon*. The mon was a crest worn on uniform and equipment in the great civil wars of the 16th century. The list that follows is not complete, but rather an attempt to show the origins and designs of some Brigade patches.

The 1st and 2nd Inf. Brigades were part of 1st Inf. Div. in World War II, but were reorganized as Airborne Brigades in summer 1943. Disbanded at the end of the War, they were reactivated as independent Infantry Brigades in 1958 and returned to 1st Inf. in 1962.

1st Inf. Bde. has a white '1' on a blue background, 2nd has a blue and a white bayonet.

Post-war Germany—Pvt, 1st Class Melin Leimons of Co. C, 1st Bn. 16th Inf. Bde. of the 1st Infantry Div. shows the working parts of an M60 to Hugo Keindengon.

2nd Armored Div (subdued)

3rd Armored Div

4th Armored Div

8th Armored Div

10th Armored Div

49th Armored Div

An M113 of M troop, 3rd Squadron, 11th Armored Cavalry Regt covers a hedge line ten miles south west of Ben Cat, South Vietnam.

High technology logistics — a soldier of the 13th (US) Support Command checks off vehicles with a light pen and a bar-coded inventory.

11th Inf. Bde. has three arrows which resemble the figure '11' and also an arrow marking a breakthrough on a map. The insignia was approved on July 1966.

29th Inf. Bde., which is part of the Hawaiian National Guard, had a patch which resembled an aiming mark or sight, but this was replaced by a blue cross. The new insignia was approved in 1968.

36th Inf. Bde. is part of the Texas National Guard and so has a lone star on a blue shield.

39th Inf. Bde., part of the Arkansas National Guard, adopted a patch in 1968 which featured a white Bowie knife on a blue and red field.

40th Armored Bde., part of the California National Guard, has the sun-burst insignia of the 40th Inf. Div., but also two lightning bolts on a blue and red field.

41st Inf. Bde. has two crossed barbed arrows or harpoons on a blue and white field. The insignia was approved in June 1969.

49th Inf. Bde. is part of the California National Guard and has a cactus rose on a yellow and blue shield with a yellow diamond.

49th Armd. Bde. is part of the Texas National Guard and has the lone star and yellow, red and blue triangle of the US Armored Corps.

The 53rd Inf. Bde., part of the Florida National Guard, was formed as an armored unit in December 1964 and became an Infantry Brigade in 1968. It has a Spanish conquistador's helmet as part of the patch, but retains the tricolored Armored Corps design.

67th Inf. Bde., part of the Nebraska National Guard, has a patch approved in June 1964, featuring a pike on a blue field.

69th Inf. Bde., Kansas National Guard. The patch was approved in December 1964 and resembles a flower in a water course.

72nd Inf. Bde., Texas National Guard, had their insignia in the colors of the State flag approved in 1968.

81st Inf. Bde., Washington National Guard, has the Indian symbol of the raven. The patch was approved in May 1970.

86th Armd. Bde. has a stag's head on the red, yellow and blue of the Armored Corps.

Men of 5th Armored Div, 46th Armd Inf. Bn. in their White halftrack named Copenhagen pass a burning building. The vehicle is loaded with stores, ammunition and captured items.

171st Inf. Bde. and 172nd Inf. Bde. are Alaskan units and both have a bayonet against snow-covered mountains. The 171st has Northern Lights above the mountains and the 172nd has the Plough or Big Dipper.

173rd Airborne had a winged bayonet with a black Airborne tab above it. During the Vietnam War this patch appeared in modified forms reflecting both unit pride and anti-authoritarian attitudes. One version with interlocked black and white fists bore the slogan 'Two Shades of Soul Togetherness', with 'The Herd' in place of the Airborne tab, while another retained 'The Herd' and replaced the winged bayonet with a winged opium pipe.

A bayonet against the silhouette of a grenade and a bayonet on a white bar were adopted by the 191st Inf. Bde. in October 1963 and 193rd Inf. Bde. in August 1963 respectively.

The 196th Inf. Bde. has the double-headed slow fuse for a matchlock musket. The insignia was adopted in October 1965.

The 197th Inf. Bde. has a red cartridge against a blue and white background.

Among the heraldic motifs of the Artillery are the 30th Bde. raised on the Ryukyus Islands which has an oriental image of three arrows symbolizing three tens, within a circle. The 38th Artillery has a mailed fist on a red and yellow field, which symbolizes the divided Korean peninsula.

The 15th and 221st Military Police Bdes. both have Griffon's heads, similar in appearance to that of the 209th Field Artillery Bde.

A cross appears in the design of the 8th, 175th, 213th and 807th Medical Bde. patches. The 15th has an inverted sword with a swathing of bandages.

■ US ARMORED DIVISIONS ■

Currently there are five Armored Divisions in the US Army — the 1st, 2nd and 3rd are Active Army units while the 49th and 50th are divisions of the Army National Guard. All Armored Divisions have the triangular patch which was adopted by the Armored Corps in World War I. It is split into red, yellow and blue — the colors of the

1st Cavalry Division

1st Cavalry (non-standard woven patch produced to
commemorate the 1st Cav's airmobile role in Vietnam)

2nd Cavalry Division

75th Inf Brigade (subdued)

173rd Inf Brigade (without Airborne tab)

75th Field Artillery Brigade (subdued)

15th M.P. Brigade

199th Inf Brigade

cavalry, infantry and artillery — component parts of all armored formations.

The lightning bolt, tank tracks and cannon on round cavalry yellow patches were the insignia of the 1st Cavalry Regt. (Mech.), 7th Cav. Regt. (Mech.) and 13th Cav. Regt. (Mech.). Other units within the 7th Mechanized Cavalry Brigade, formed in 1937, had their arm colors as backing to the patch — so mechanized artillery and ordnance had red, and the medical troop, purple.

When the Armored Force was formed on July 10, 1940 its insignia, which was authorized on May 7, 1941, combined the triangular patch of the Armored Corps with that of the 7th Mechanized Cavalry Brigade in the center. Roman numerals were to have been positioned at the apex of each patch to distinguish each Corps. These were short-lived, with I Corps being disbanded after the landings in Sicily in 1943 and II, III, and IV Corps becoming the 18th, 19th and 20th Army Corps respectively. There were no V to XVIII Corps, though patches were made.

In World War II, Armored Division patches were made numbering from 1 to 22, though 17, 18, 19 and 21 did not exist. The National Guard Armored Divisions adopted numbers 27, 30, 40, 48, 49 and 50.

An M1 Abrams tank deployed on Reforger 82 in West Germany. The US Cavalry traded in their horses for tanks before World War II and the Abrams is the most modern MBT to enter service with Cavalry and Armored units.

The 1st Armd. Div. (Old Ironsides) fought in Europe in World War II and is an Active Army division with its HQ at Ansbach, West Germany, though the bulk of the division is at Fort Hood, in the US. Its equipment was used to reform the 1st Cavalry Div. in 1970-71 following the withdrawal of 1st Cav. from Vietnam. The 1st Armd. Div. in turn took on the equipment of the disbanded 4th.

The 2nd Armd. Div. (Hell on Wheels) fought in Europe in World War II and is an Active Army division based at Fort Hood, Texas after its return from Europe in 1946. It is the only armored division in the US Army to remain in continuous service since its activation. Under the command of General George S. Patton it earned its nickname 'Hell on Wheels'. It fought in the Battle of the Bulge after a 75-mile drive in ice and snow. As part of III Corps is returns to Europe on Reforger Exercises and was the first division to receive the M1 tank and Bradley fighting vehicle.

The 3rd Armd. Div. (Spearhead) fought in Europe. It is an active army unit which has been stationed in Frankfurt,

US Marines during peace-keeping operations in Lebanon wear a Stars and Stripes patch on their BDUs. The wearing of the national flag dates back to World War II, as the most obvious method of distinguishing US from other Allied forces.

West Germany since the 1950s.

The 49th Armd. Div. (Lone Star) has been called 'the largest division in NATO'. It is part of the Army National Guard based at Austin, Texas and was Federalized during the 1961 Berlin crisis. It has a star between the words 'Lone' and 'Star' on the title on its patch.

The 50th Armd. Div. (Jersey Blues) is part of the Army National Guard based at Somerset, New Jersey. Its divisional name is not displayed at the base of the patch as with the other armored divisions.

A prototype armored division is currently being planned for the US Army and it will be interesting to see which of the armored or cavalry divisions are reactivated for this role.

All the armored divisions fought in Europe in World War II. Their titles, which were largely embroidered with black letters on cavalry yellow, also appeared with yellow on khaki and blue with yellow letters. The titles reflect the violence and drive of armored warfare; 1st — Old Ironside, 2nd — Hell on Wheels, 3rd — Spearhead, 4th — Break-

through, 5th — Victory, 6th — Super Sixth, 7th — Lucky 7th. The 8th was known as Iron Duce, Iron Snake and also Thundering Herd. The 9th changed from Phantom to Remagen after its successful *coup de main* at Remagen bridge on the Rhine in 1945. The 10th was known as Tiger, the 11th as Thunderbolt, the 12th as Hellcat, and also Speed is the Password, though whether this latter title appeared on a patch must beg the question of how it could be fitted in. The 13th was called Blackcat; the 14th, Liberator; the 27th, Empire and the 30th Dixie and Volunteers — the latter title is flanked by a miniature of the Roman XXX of the 30th Infantry Division. The 40th had the title Grizzly; the 48th, Hurricane; the 49th, Lone Star and the 50th, Jersey Blues.

The tricolored triangular armored patch also serves as the basis for armored personnel in GHQ, 3rd Armored Division Reconnaissance, with the letters RCN, Demonstration Regiment — DR, 7th Army Tank Training Center — TTC, 17th Armored Group — 17GP, 510th Armored Reconnaissance Battalion — 510 RECON, 7th Cavalry Regiment — 7 CAV. The most fascinating is the patch worn by a special armored unit which was in training for the invasion of Japan — it was an unnumbered armor patch with an Airborne tab above it.

ABOVE The 2nd Armd. Div. — Hell on Wheels — on
Exercise Certain Strike, part of Reforger 87. A Spec 4 in
the turret of his M1 Abrams main battle tank.

TOP Dressed in camouflaged BDUs (battle dress utilities),
a US Army officer talks to a Dutch officer. The subdued US
Army Vietnam patch can be seen on his right shoulder
indicating service in Vietnam.

CHAPTER FOUR

OPERATIONAL THEATERS, COMMANDS, SUPPORT SERVICES AND TRAINING SCHOOLS

US Army medics work on a casualty on Utah Beach on
June 6, 1944. They have the universally recognised Red
Cross insignia, though the divisional patch on the
casualty (who is also a medic) has been removed by the
censor.

■ THEATERS, COMMANDS ■ AND SUPPORT SERVICES

During World War II a range of patches was produced for the different war theaters, commands and training establishments. Often, these were as symbolic as many of the heraldic devices on divisional patches.

The Army Ground Forces included representations of the Armored Corps patch for the Armored Center, a glider and parachute for the Airborne Command, and the British Combined Operations motif of Eagle, Anchor and Tommy Gun for Amphibious Forces. The British design was in red on a black background.

US Army Amphibious Units adopted the patch in yellow on blue, while Combined Operations retained the original design. A ship's wheel on a red shield was used for Ports of Embarkation. The Engineer Amphibious Command had a small seahorse within an oval patch, while Bomb Disposal had a aircraft bomb shape similar to the British patch. Tank destroyer units had a snarling black panther flanked by tracks. Without the tracks and slightly modified, the motif was to reappear as the patch of the Vietnamese Rangers (Biet Dong Ouan) in the 1960s and 70s.

The Frontier Defense Sectors were manned by the coastal artillery and had a series of patches in red and yellow on a khaki background. These included the 1st Coastal Artillery (New England), 2nd (New York — Philadelphia), 3rd (Chesapeake Bay), 4th (Southern Coastal) and 9th (Pacific Coastal). Hawaii, which after Pearl Harbor was more threatened than the mainland US seaboard, had two patches for Coastal Defense and the Coastal Artillery Brigade. Anti-aircraft Defense had patches using the same colors but with arrows in place of the shell motif. The Anti-Aircraft Command had the letters 'AA' in red on white within a blue bordered circle. There were AA Artillery Commands for the Central, Southern and Eastern United States.

The Army Ground Forces had a simple circular patch in red, white and blue and yellow, red and blue for the Replacement and School Command. The Army Service Forces (ASF) had a blue star within a white octofoil patch with a red border. The ASF provided service and support for the army both in the United States and later overseas.

The World War II patch of US Armed Forces Pacific Ocean Area theater depicted the twelve stars of the Southern Cross constellation. The Southern Cross on its own was adopted by US Army Forces in the South Atlantic — however this patch also included the silhouette of Ascension Island rising from a green ocean.

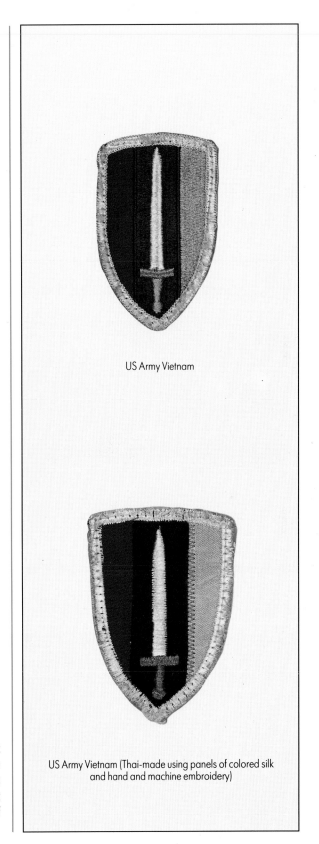

US Army Vietnam

US Army Vietnam (Thai-made using panels of colored silk and hand and machine embroidery)

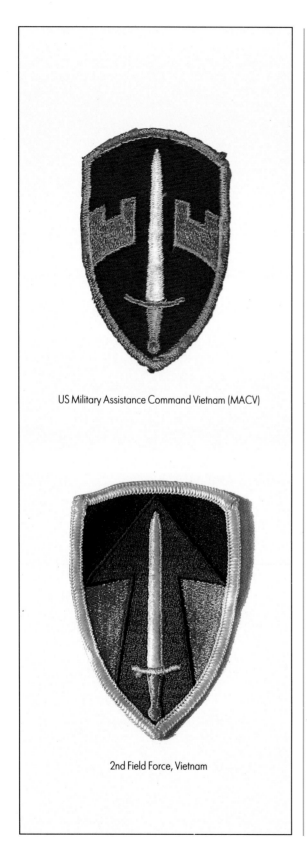

US Military Assistance Command Vietnam (MACV)

2nd Field Force, Vietnam

The ETO — European Theater of Operations — had two patches. Both featured an arrow bursting through chains symbolizing Nazi occupation. The Advanced Base patch had within it a miniature of the Army Service Forces patch.

A Moorish dome enclosing a star was adopted for North Africa. Perhaps the most widely known theater patch is the CBI — China-Burma-India — shield with its Nationalist Chinese sun and US star. It is a patch often associated with leather flight jackets of the US Flying Tigers pilots who operated in support of the Nationalist Chinese forces. The 5307th Composite Unit, widely known as Merrill's Marauders which operated in Burma with British and Chinese, forces also used the Sun and Star design. There were a number of patches which also included a red lightning bolt on a shield quartered in blue and black. The CBI patch was to survive after the War as the MAAG Formosa patch, with the letters MAAG in place of the US star. Men working on the Ledo or Burma road had a patch depicting the road winding through mountains towards a Chinese sun, above on a red bar were three stars. US forces in the Middle East had a star on a red field above two wavy blue lines.

The Supreme Headquarters Allied Expeditionary Forces, worn in North West Europe by personnel on General Eisenhower's staff, showed a flaming sword penetrating the darkness of Occupied Europe with a rainbow band of color and a pale blue band. After the War the design was retained for the US Army Europe, but dark blue was substituted for black. With the tab 'Berlin' it was worn by the Berlin Brigade. The sword and rainbow appeared in the patch of the US Military Liaison Mission Potsdam, though with the addition of the Stars and Stripes.

Allied Forces HQ had the letters 'AF' on a blue circle, with a red border. The General HQ South West Pacific showed the letters 'GHQ' on a standard against a khaki field.

The US Mission to Moscow had a representation of the American eagle and shield with 'America' in cyrilic script above it.

Base and Defense commands were respectively located overseas and in the US. Base commands were to protect the United States in war, though the London Base Command, which featured Big Ben and the letters 'LBC', was principally involved in work on the Second Front.

The Iceland Base Command showed an iceberg with the tip showing red above the sea; the Greenland Command, sea and ice in blue and white lines. The Caribbean Defense Command showing a galleon in full sail lives on as the 33rd Infantry Combat team patch with the tab 33rd Infantry. The same patch with the tab 'Jungle Ex-

Military Advisory Assistance Group — Laos (also produced in black)

US Army Special Forces

Special Forces (subdued)

Airborne, Recondo and Special Forces tabs in full color and subdued.

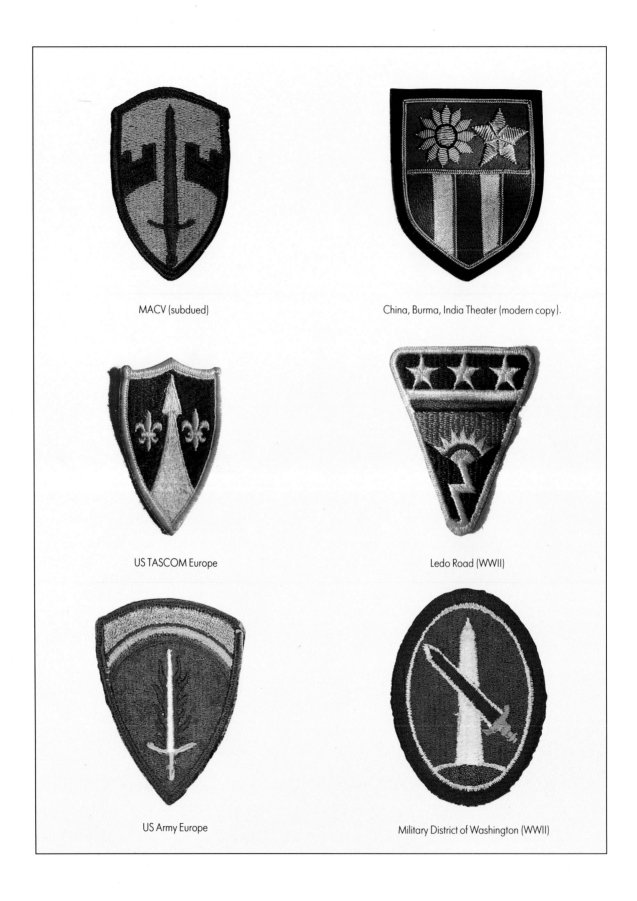

MACV (subdued)

China, Burma, India Theater (modern copy).

US TASCOM Europe

Ledo Road (WWII)

US Army Europe

Military District of Washington (WWII)

A 155mm self-propelled gun is used against a German bunker on the Siegfried line in November 1944. The impact of the big shells with super quick fuzes was devastating when they hit the bunkers.

pert' is awarded to men who have completed the course run by the Jungle Warfare Training Center at Fort Sherman, Panama Canal Zone, which was set up in the 1950s. With the colors reversed as a blue ship on a white patch the same design was adopted by the School of the Americas — the US sponsored civil and military training establishment for officers from Central and South America.

The Military District of Washington patch is oval with the Washington Memorial and a red sword. It was part of the Army Service Forces.

Men attending the Officers Candidates School had a simple patch with the letters 'S' and 'C' interlocked and enclosed by an 'O'. The Army Specialized Training Program and Reserve trained young men in colleges and schools. The Reserve Officers Training Corps, ROTC, had three patches. The first design was a shield, changed in the 1950s to a red, white and blue patch with the torch of knowledge. The current design has a sword against a representation of classical columns. Since the war ROTCs have developed a range of individual college patches.

In World War II there were individual commands which included the US Army in Alaska, where troops wore patches with polar bears and seals. The rather attractive cartoon seal on the Alaskan Defense Command, with the Aurora Borealis, was changed to a more aggressive snarling polar bear when the Command was transformed into a Department.

The Antilles Department had a turret from a Spanish fort in red and yellow, the colors of the Spanish flag. The Panama Department had the portcullis of the Panama Hellgate and a shield device suggesting the isthmus that joins North and South America. The Philippine Department had an armed sealion, and Hawaii an 'H' configured like an Oriental *mon*.

After World War II, occupation produced its own patches. The Berlin District had the Brandenburg Gate on an orange shield. Troops in Trieste, the disputed port on the Italian/Yugoslav border, had a modified version of the 88th Division patch with the town crest in the center and a tab reading 'Trust' above it. US troops in Austria had the Tactical Command patch and the US Forces

Brass on parade — their patches are either European (Advanced Base) or S.H.A.E.F. The officers in the front row have several medals and overseas service stripes and even the wound stripes from World War I on their cuffs.

Austria, which used the Austrian colors of red and white with a sword and a branch of laurel. There were two versions, one with the words 'Austria' and 'US' on a square patch, the other without letters on a classic shield shape. One of the more intriguing patches is the US Allied Control Command Hungary — this was a shield with the words 'America US ACC Magyarorszag'.

The US TASCOM Europe, which was set up in France on April 25, 1953, features a French fleur-de-lis and an arrow representing the flow of supplies. On August 6, 1964 it was renamed US Army Communications Zone, Europe and on September 26, 1969 it became US Theater Army Support Command, Europe.

The war crimes trials in Japan and Nuremberg, Germany produced their own patches. Both featured the scales of justice, though the Japanese trials had in addition a lightning bolt crossed with an oriental sword.

US Forces in the Far East had a circular patch showing a snow-capped Mt Fuji, topped off with a black tab '29th RCT Raiders' when the patch was later used by the 29th Regimental Combat Team. The Ryukus Command based in Okinawa had a yellow Torii gate on a black patch. The Japan Logistics Command had the letters 'JLC' in a mock Oriental script, while the West Pacific Far East Command adopted the wartime Army Service Forces patch with a lightning bolt and five smaller stars like the Southern Cross. Guam base had two patches, the first had the word 'Guam' on a patch showing a palm tree and a sailing boat. When the Mariannas, Bonin, Guam Command was formed the patch was changed to a single palm tree — perhaps the old patch was a little too like an image from a holiday brochure.

The growth of US involvement in South East Asia after World War II produced patches for the Military Assistance Advisory Group, MAAG. It was a blue patch with twelve white stars and resembled the 508th Airborne Infantry Regiment patch, except that the 508th was based on the 82nd Airborne patch with a red square and an Airborne tab. There were MAAGs in Laos, Formosa, Thailand and Vietnam. In Vietnam the increase in US involvement in the 1960s and the creation of the Military Assistance Command, Vietnam, MACV, produced a patch showing a white sword on a red shield breaking through an arched 'embattled fess' — a heraldic fortified wall. MACV pro-

Pacific Ocean Area (WWII)

European (Advanced Base) (WWII)

Aleutian Islands Command

North Africa (WWII)

US Army Forces Western Pacific

Berlin District

Alaska Support Command

Army Amphibian Units (WWII)

Airborne Command

1st Allied Airborne Army

1st Special Service Force

Army Ground Forces

A Lieutenant of Engineers (the castle insignia is on his coat) with the shoulder patch of the Army Service Forces on his jacket admires a Renoir in the Louvre.

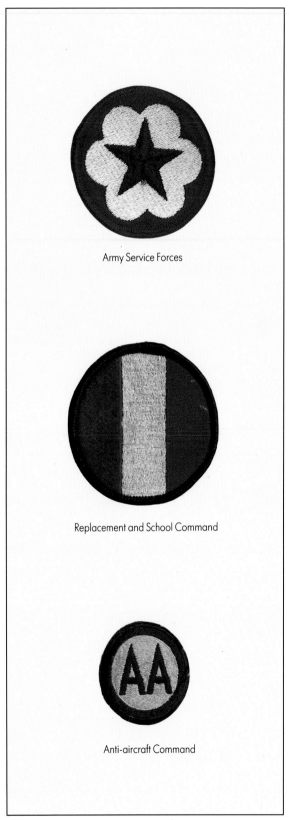

Army Service Forces

Replacement and School Command

Anti-aircraft Command

duced a *Staff Memorandum 670-1* which read: 'Yellow and red are the Republic of Vietnam colors. The red ground alludes to the infiltration and oppression from beyond the embattled wall (i.e. The Great Wall of China). The opening in the wall through which this infiltration and oppression flow is blocked by the sword representing US military aid and support. The wall is arched and the sword pointed upward in reference to the offensive action pushing the aggressor back.'

The US Army Vietnam adopted a shield divided vertically into yellow, blue and red with a sword in the central blue section. Yellow and red were the colors of the Republic of Vietnam, though some observers talked about the yellow and red 'hordes' of North Vietnam and China. The 1st and 2nd Field Force in Vietnam had variants of the US Army Vietnam patch. The three colors were common to both as was the vertical sword, though 1st Field Force had a battle-axe-shaped patch and the 2nd incorporated a blue arrow thrusting into a red field.

Officers and men of the 82nd Airborne arrive in Paris for R and R in World War II. The man second from the left has paratrooper's wings on his tunic. The men have the patch of glider-borne paratroops on their forage caps. Their high Corcoran boots further identify them as paratroops.

Vietnam saw the growth of informal patches for divisional sniper and reconnaissance teams and even commemorative patches, like the one produced for men who participated in the Son Tay raid on November 21, 1970. The Special Forces, with their distinctive green beret and its colored cloth badge backings and 'Saigon Electrical Works' patch of a sword with three lightning bolts, achieved a considerable military cachet and sense of mystique in the South-East Asian theater.

With patches came a variety of shoulder tabs in colors which imitated the prized Ranger tab. Some said simply 'Sniper', 'Commando', 'Scout Dog', 'Scout', 'Tracker' or 'Combat Artists', though others boasted 'Sons of Bitche', 'Sheep', 'Clowns' or, rather chillingly, 'Funeral Squad'. Kit Carson Scouts, Vietcong or North Vietnamese who had surrendered to the US Army and opted to join them as scouts, had their own patch.

Helicopter airmobility in Vietnam produced variants on some older cavalry patches as 1st Cavalry became 'Airmobile'. The patches, as with other 'informal' insignia, were usually worn on the left pocket. There are over 200 recorded specialist or 'elite' patches and insignia generated by the Vietnam War and they have been the subject of books in their own right.

■ SCHOOLS, TRAINING ■ CENTERS AND TRAINING COURSES

The Military Academy at West Point is probably the most widely known training establishment in the US Army. Its

Army Materiel Command

1st Logistical Command

Army Reserve Officers Training Corps

Combat Developments Command

Engineer Center and School

Corps of Engineers

Infantry School

Jungle School (cadre) (subdued)

O.C.S. (Female)

Aviation School

Signal Corps Center and School

Caribbean Defence Command

An officer and a gentleman — Officer-Cadet Hunn and his partner at the Class of 1970 'Ring Hop' at the West Point Military Academy. The giant ring represents the Academy Graduation ring favored by officers in the US Army — as such it is an informal item of insignia.

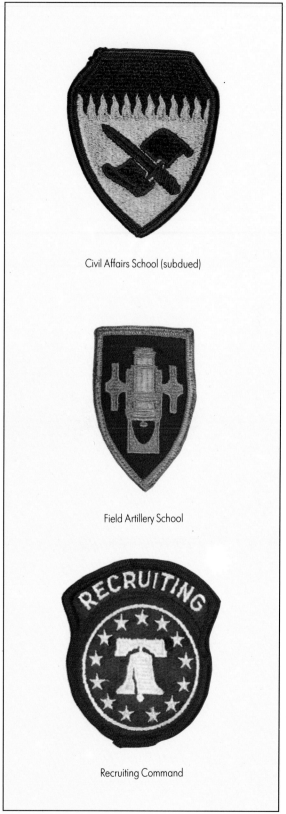

Civil Affairs School (subdued)

Field Artillery School

Recruiting Command

patch features a classical Greek helmet on a gray and black shield. Two versions exist: the cadre patch has an oblique black bar, while the US Military Academy has the shield divided into quarters.

A man's cotton shirt, sateen OG 107 with a DSA number indicating a manufacture date in 1967 in the author's collection has an interesting combination of patches. The owner, Lt Moran, an infantry officer in the 199th Inf. Brigade (Light), served operationally in Vietnam where the Brigade was deployed between 1966 and 1970. He won the Combat Infantry Badge. Most intriguingly he then went to serve on the cadre of the US Military Academy — presumably as an experienced young infantry officer on the administrative staff. The shirt is also unusual in having a subdued inked name tag, subdued embroidered rank and CIB, but an earlier black and gold US Army tab and full color patches.

Before any training can be undertaken by a soldier he has to be recruited or drafted into the army. The US Army Recruiting Service initially had a shield-shaped patch which was later changed to a square and then to

A different sort of insignia — OPFOR, the pseudo-soviet forces who are the enemy at the National Training Center, Fort Irwin, California. They have characteristic black berets and insignia like that of the Soviet Army — the vehicle is a modified Sheridan light tank.

A photographer of the US Army Combat Pictorial Division with the Strategic Communications Command patch adjusts his equipment during an exercise in 1988. As a lower priority unit he has not yet reached the Kevlar 'Fritz' helmet and so still wears the GI 'pot'.

an oval design. The square and oval patches show the Liberty Bell surrounded by the 13 stars of the first States of the Union.

Staff and students at training establishments in the United States, Europe and Asia had patches which indicated that they were either graduates or part of the training team. Patches or tabs fostered a mystique and a competitive edge. The Infantry School has a bayonet on an infantry blue background with the motto 'Follow Me'.

The US Intelligence Command has the Sphinx on a pale blue background, while the Intelligence Agency has a rose in blue and gray. The rose is also used by the British Army Intelligence Corps. The US Army Engineer Technical Intelligence Team has the castle of the Corps of Engineers. The Field Artillery School has a vertical view of a cannon on a red shield. The Artillery and Missile School

has the black outline of a missile superimposed on the shield. The Army War College has the torch of knowledge on a black shield with three stars; the Command and General Staff School, Fort Leavenworth, has three oil lamps with an inverted 'V'.

The patch which attracted most sarcastic comment was the Special Warfare School insignia, which was likened to a cooking pot. It is a shield with a three-flamed lamp backed by the crossed arrows of the Special Forces.

The Fixed Wing Aviation and Helicopter Schools have, respectively, a blue shield with a red observation aircraft, and a red shield with a black Sikorsky helicopter. The Aviation School has a winged torch, similar in design to the 173rd Airborne and 1st Aviation Brigade.

The Judge Advocate General School has a sword and quill pen with the torch and laurel wreath. The Civil

Tank Destroyer Forces

Special Warfare School

107th Transportation Brigade

107th A.C.R

67th Inf Brigade

197th Inf Brigade

Affairs School patch features a sword and scroll.

The 'Enemy' force for soldiers in training centers in the 1950s in the United States was originally composed of men in the 'Aggressor Force'. They had a patch showing a green triangle inside a circle. Following Vietnam, there was a serious re-evaluation of training and Opposing Forces, or OPFOR, were established at the National Training Center, Fort Irwin. OPFOR wear a version of Soviet uniforms and use real Eastern Bloc or modified US vehicles. They have a patch showing a black star on a green circle. Staff at the National Training Center have a patch which has the red, yellow and blue of artillery, cavalry and infantry.

A diamond in Army or Corps colors, with the torch of knowledge and Corps insignia or a version of it, has been adopted by ten US Army Centers and Schools. They are: Missile & Munitions, Military Intelligence, Military Police, Ordnance, Chemical Corps, Transportation, Medical, Quartermaster, Signal Corps and Engineer.

Specialized units and training courses run at divisional level often feature a variation of the divisional patch. However, the 2nd Infantry Division Rangers School features a map of Korea with the North in red and South in white. A Spec 4s OD shirt in the author's collection has the shirt pocket patch with the 2nd Division Indian head on the left sleeve. The Ranger Patch features an Indian head on an arrow pointing northward with the motto 'Imjin Scouts'. The 5th Division Recondo School has a black Roman 'V' with the motto 'Recondo'.

2nd Infantry come ashore in Korea in 1963. The Indian Head Division has been resident in Korea since the end of the Korean War.

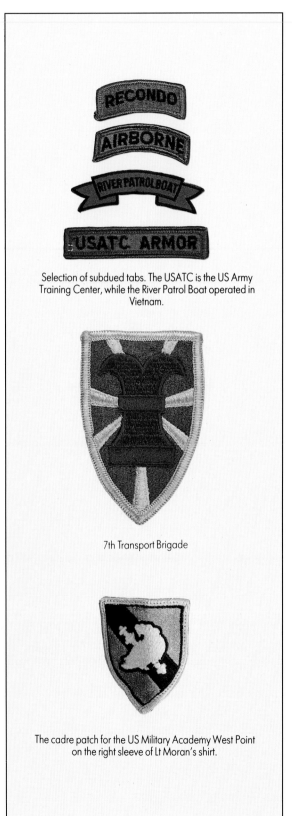

Selection of subdued tabs. The USATC is the US Army Training Center, while the River Patrol Boat operated in Vietnam.

7th Transport Brigade

The cadre patch for the US Military Academy West Point on the right sleeve of Lt Moran's shirt.

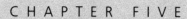

CHAPTER FIVE

THE UNITED STATES
ARMY AIR FORCE

A USAAF B-17 bomber with nose art of the Commander
in Chief of the Allied Forces—Ike.

A Staff Sergeant of the US Army Air Force 9th Air Force turns on the charm with the mother of his Parisian date in 1944.

Prior to 1947, when the USAF was established as a separate force, it was, as the United States Army Air Force, part of the US Army. It had begun life in 1907 as three men in the Army Signal Corps. In 1926 it was designated the Air Corps, having earned its wings in World War I. In World War II the Corps was reorganized in June 1941 and was designated the Army Air Force. The 1st, 2nd, 3rd and 4th Air Forces were Continental Air Forces which were tasked with the defense of the United States. The Combat Air Forces were activated in strategic areas of operation and their unit patches were to become the outward signs of the USAAF's overseas power projection.

The old USAAF patch was an oriental-style design which also resembled a turning propellor blade. The 'new' patch used the pre-War USAAF white star with a circular center which was painted on USAAF aircraft. The patch had a blue background with yellow wings. Most of the USAAF patches were circular on a blue background; exceptions were the 2nd Air Force (square), the 6th (six sided), the 11th (shield), the 12th (inverted triangle), the

US Strategic Air Force and the Desert Air Force (shields).

The 1st Air Force had the figure '1' above the patch, the 2nd an eagle with a star, the 3rd a figure '3', the 4th a winged star and four radiating gold bars. The 5th had five stars, with the figure '5' and the star as a meteor. It was originally the Philippine Department Air Force and was activated in May 1941. It was redesignated the 5th Air Force in 1942 and supported landings on Guadalcanal and Admiralty Islands and saw air action in New Guinea.

The 6th, which had a winged star with the silhouette of a galleon above it, was the Panama Canal Air Force. It was responsible for defense of the strategically-important Canal Zone and for anti-submarine operations in the Gulf of Mexico. The galleon motif has remained in use in the US Army.

The 7th had a star pierced by a figure '7'. It originated as the Hawaiian Air Force and was redesignated the 7th

1st Air Force   3rd Air Force

in February 1942. It covered the Hawaiian Islands and became the principal striking force in the Central Pacific.

The 8th, 'The Mighty 8th', was the striking force against Germany and Occupied Europe and was based in the United Kingdom. Its B-17 bombers and Mustang fighters made deep penetration raids into Germany. It had a winged '8' which enclosed the USAAF star.

The 9th had the figure '9' in red on a gold circle with white wings topped by the USAAF star. The 9th was activated in April 1942 and served in the Middle East. After the North African campaign it was transferred to the United Kingdom to support operations in Europe. The 9th became one of the largest Tactical Air Forces in the world.

The 10th had the figure '10' with gold wings topped by the USAAF star. The 10th was activated in 1942 and operated against Japanese supply lines in Burma and in the defense of China and India.

The 11th Air Force had the figure '11' with a USAAF star with a single wing. The 11th, which had been the Alaskan Air Force, was redesignated in February 1942. It saw action in the North Pacific at Dutch Harbor, the Aleutian Islands and in long-range bombing missions against the Kurile Islands.

The 12th had the figure '12' within a winged star. It was activated in August 1942 and operated as a Tactical Air Force in support of ground troops in North Africa and the invasion of Europe.

The 13th had a winged star with '13' above. Activated in January 1943 it provided air defense of supply routes in the South Pacific and tactical air support of land and sea operations in the Solomon Islands.

The 14th was known as the China Air Task Force and, before that, The Flying Tigers. They sported a winged tiger with the USAAF star. The 14th was activated in July 1942 under command of the 10th and then became an Air Force in its own right in March 1943. It was tasked with the defense of China and with attacks on Japanese lines of communication in Burma.

The 15th had a patch similar to the 13th, but had the figure '15' in yellow thread. It was activated in November 1943 as a strategic Air Force in the Mediterranean Allied Air Force. It was involved in long-range bombing operations against Germany.

RIGHT Following the airborne assault in the Rhine crossings, a US paratrooper with the bayonet fixed on his Garand moves towards a billowing cargo parachute.

5th Air Force

7th Air Force

9th Air Force

13th Air Force

Airborne Troop Carrier

11th Air Force

The 20th had a globe motif over the winged star and figure '20'. It was activated in 1944 for very long-range strategic bombing operations in the Far East against Japan. There were also tactical or strategic Air Forces within Area of Operation Air Forces. They were joint commands by the USAAF or British RAF.

The Desert Air Force had a winged 8th Army shield with a bar bearing an RAF roundel and USAAF star. The 9th and 12th Air Forces operated in conjunction with the RAF in North Africa.

The Mediterranean Allied Air Force grew out of the Desert Air Force and the 12th Air Force and was tasked with supporting the invasion of Sicily. The patch was an unusual shape, being four-sided, with white wings above the letters MAAF on wavy pale blue lines.

The US Strategic Air Force Europe was activated in January 1944, combining the 8th and 15th Air Forces into a powerful force in the long-range war against Germany. It had a shield-shaped patch with a winged star and the letters 'USSTAF'.

The Air Training Command grew out of the amalgamation of the Technical Training Command and the Flying Training Command in July 1943. The patch consisted of a winged white star pierced by the torch of knowledge. The Air Transport Command, activated in April 1941 as the Ferry Command, was redesignated in 1942 and had two sections, Ferrying and Air Transport. The patch showed a half globe, but did not have the USAAF star. A separate gold-colored patch was produced for Air Transport Command Ground Personnel.

Troop Carrier Command had a huge eagle carrying an armed man. Its role was to train troop carrier and glider crews, and the evacuation of the wounded.

The Airborne Troop Carrier had a shield incorporating the Airborne tab as well as the words 'Troop Carrier' and a USAAF star suspended on a parachute with wings. It transported airborne forces and stores in combat.

Perhaps one of the most fascinating patches was that for The Manhattan Project, the secret project to build the atomic bomb which was under the command of USAAF General Groves. It shows a gold atom being split by a white bolt coming from another which bears the USAAF star.

Specialists had blue inverted triangle patches which showed a camera (Air Force Photography Specialist), a wind vane (AF Weather Specialist), a gear wheel (AF Engineering Specialist), a radio mast (AF Communications Specialist) and a bomb (AF Armature Specialist).

US Army Air Force

USAAF 8th Air Force

INDEX

■ BIBLIOGRAPHY ■

The following books have been invaluable in the preparation of this work:

Shoulder Patch Insignia of the United States Armed Forces Wolf Appleton. New York.

US Military Shoulder Patches of the United States Armed Forces 4th Edition. Jack Britton and George Washington Jr. Tulsa Oklahoma.

Air Force Collecting Cliff Gates. M.C.N. Press, Tulsa, Oklahoma.

Elite Unit Insignia of the Vietnam War Leroy Thomson. Arms and Armour Press, London, UK.

US Army Cloth Insignia 1941 to the Present Brian L. Davis. Arms and Armour Press, London, UK.

Army Badges and Insignia of World War 2 Guido Rosignolli. Blandford, UK.

Army Badges and Insignia Since 1945 Guido Rosignolli. Blandford, UK.